anythink

D0883266

math standards workout

SYMBOLS AND ALGEBRA

50 MATH SUPER PUZZLES

By Thomas Canavan

rosen publishing's
rosen
central®

Introduction

Why do you need this book?

Whether you are skilled with symbols or agonize over algebra, there is always room for improvement. This book is a kind of mental gym for those parts of your brain involved in thinking about symbols and algebra. These puzzles will help you to build up a variety of different math skills. They will further stretch you in the areas where you are most confident and bring you up to speed in those areas where you are weakest.

How will this book help you at school?

Symbols and Algebra complements the National Council of Teachers of Mathematics (NCTM) framework of Math Standards, providing an engaging enhancement of the curriculum in the following areas:

> *Algebra: Understand Patterns, Relations, and Functions*
> *Algebra: Represent and Analyze Mathematical Situations and Structures Using Algebraic Symbols*

Why have we chosen these puzzles?

This *Math Standards Workout* title features a range of interesting and absorbing puzzle types, challenging students to master the following skills to arrive at solutions:

- Represent, analyze, and generalize a variety of patterns with tables, graphs, words, and, when possible, symbolic rules: e.g. Symbol Math, Number Path

- Relate and compare different forms of representation for a relationship: e.g. Circling In, Number Crunch

- Develop confidence in choosing symbols and variables to help solve problems using all the mathematical operations: e.g. One to Nine, Total Concentration, and Making Arrangements

NOTE TO READERS

If you have borrowed this book from a school or classroom library, please respect other students and DO NOT write your answers in the book. Always write your answers on a separate sheet of paper.

Tile Twister

Place the eight tiles into the puzzle grid so that all adjacent numbers on each tile match up. Tiles may be rotated through 360 degrees, but none may be flipped over. Write your answers on a separate sheet of paper.

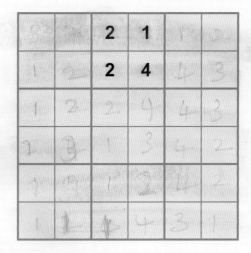

4	4
2	3

3	4
1	2

4	1
3	2

1	1
3	2

1	3
2	2

1	1
4	2

4	3
4	1

3	2
2	1

Symbol Math

Each symbol stands for a different number. In order to reach the correct total at the end of each row and column, what is the value of the circle, pentagon, square, and star? Write your answers on a separate sheet of paper.

2

○		⬠	★	= 19
⬛	★		○	= 14
	⬛	○		= 7
○	⬠		⬠	= 20
= 11	= 18	= 12	= 19

3

★	⬠	○	○	= 12
★	○	⬛	⬛	= 21
★	⬠	⬛	○	= 18
○	⬛	⬠	⬠	= 20
= 11	= 20	= 23	= 17

Circling In

The three empty circles should contain the symbols +, –, and x in some order, to make a series that leads to the number in the middle. Each symbol must be used once and calculations are made in a clockwise direction. Write your answers on a separate sheet of paper.

4

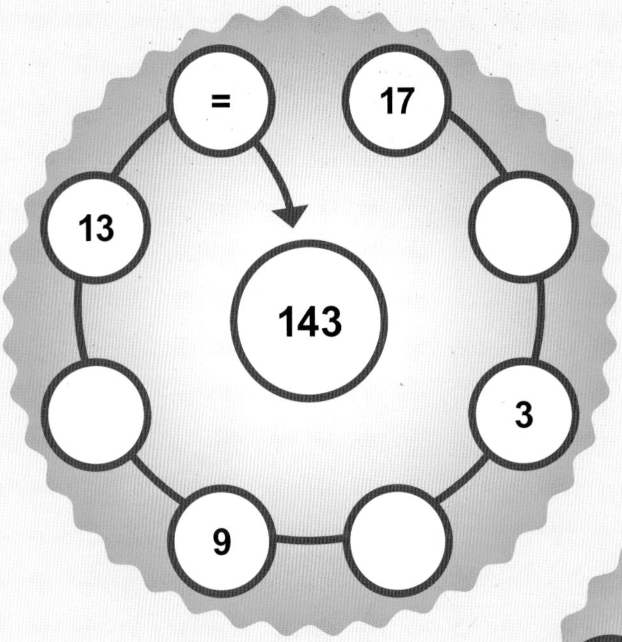

= 17

13

143

3

9

5

= 14

17

100

8

5

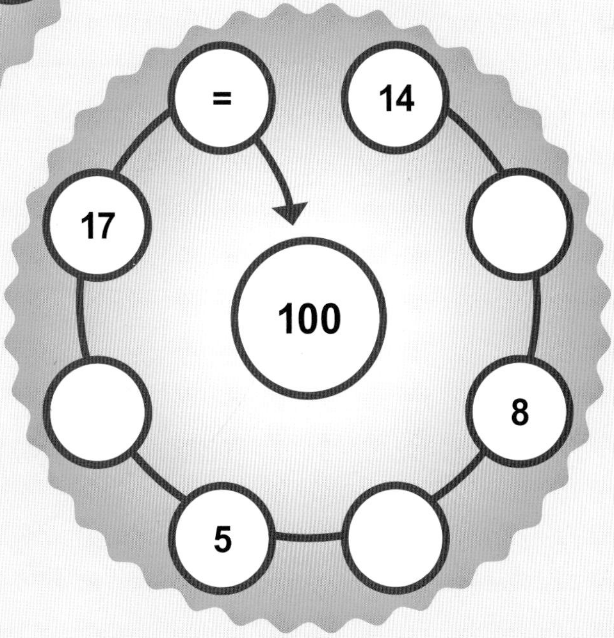

Number Path

Copy out this puzzle. Working from one square to another, horizontally or vertically (never diagonally), draw paths to pair up each set of two matching numbers. No path may be shared, and none may enter a square containing a number or part of another path. Write your answers on a separate sheet of paper.

6

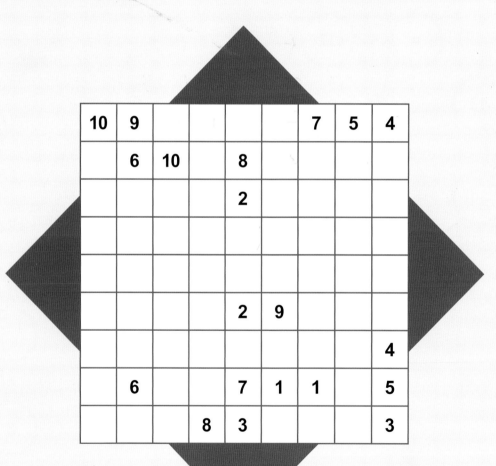

10	9					7	5	4
	6	10		8				
			2					
			2	9				
								4
	6			7	1	1		5
		8	3					3

Hexagony

Can you place the hexagons into the grid, so that where any hexagon touches another along a straight line, the number in both triangles is the same? No rotation of any hexagon is allowed! Write your answers on a separate sheet of paper.

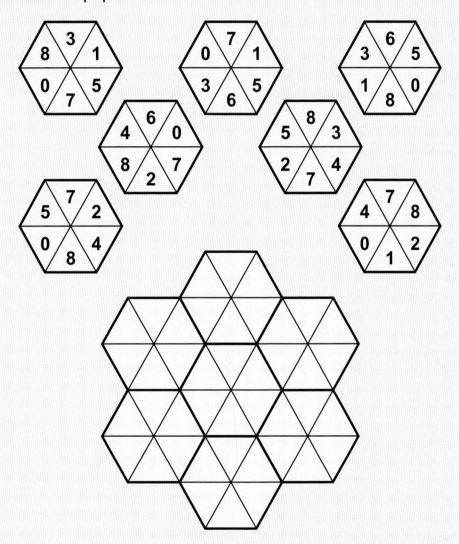

Symbol Math

Each symbol stands for a different number. In order to reach the correct total at the end of each row and column, what is the value of the circle, pentagon, square, and star? Write your answers on a separate sheet of paper.

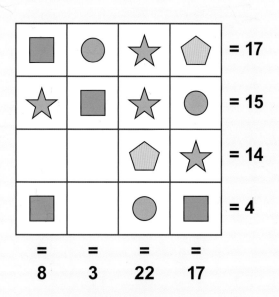

What's the Number?

In the diagram below, what number should replace the question mark? Write your answer on a separate sheet of paper.

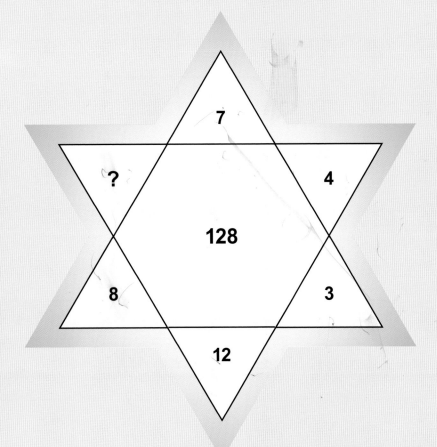

Tile Twister

Place the eight tiles into the puzzle grid so that all adjacent numbers on each tile match up. Tiles may be rotated through 360 degrees, but none may be flipped over. Write your answers on a separate sheet of paper.

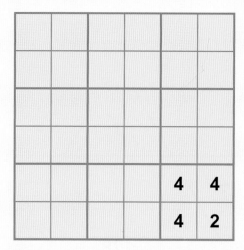

4	2		3	2		4	4		3	1
1	1		1	2		3	2		4	1

4	4		2	4		2	3		4	1
3	1		1	3		3	2		1	2

Symbol Math

Each symbol stands for a different number. In order to reach the correct total at the end of each row and column, what is the value of the circle, pentagon, square, and star? Write your answers on a separate sheet of paper.

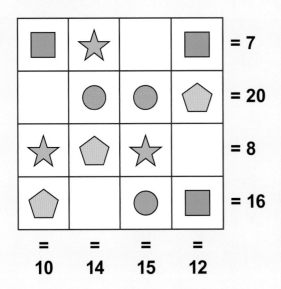

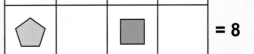

One to Nine

Using the numbers one to nine, complete these six equations (three reading across and three reading downward). Every number is used once only, and one is already in place. Write your answers on a separate sheet of paper.

1 2 3 4 5 6 7 8 9

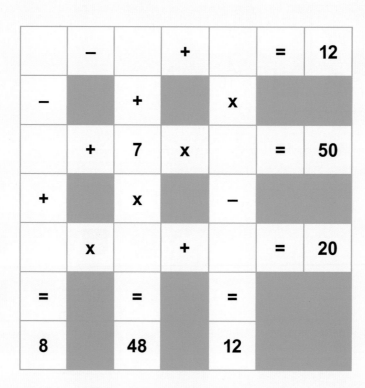

Hexagony

Can you place the hexagons into the grid, so that where any hexagon touches another along a straight line, the number in both triangles is the same? No rotation of any hexagon is allowed! Write your answers on a separate sheet of paper.

Symbol Math

Each symbol stands for a different number. In order to reach the correct total at the end of each row and column, what is the value of the circle, pentagon, square, and star? Write your answers on a separate sheet of paper.

16

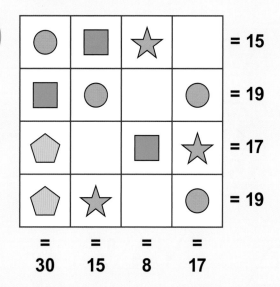

17

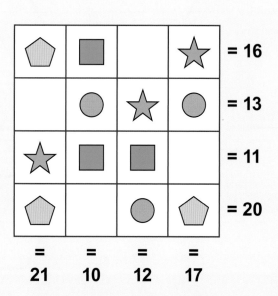

Hexagony

Can you place the hexagons into the grid, so that where any hexagon touches another along a straight line, the number in both triangles is the same? No rotation of any hexagon is allowed! Write your answers on a separate sheet of paper.

Circling In

The three empty circles should contain the symbols +, –, and x in some order, to make a series that leads to the number in the middle. Each symbol must be used once and calculations are made in a clockwise direction. Write your answers on a separate sheet of paper.

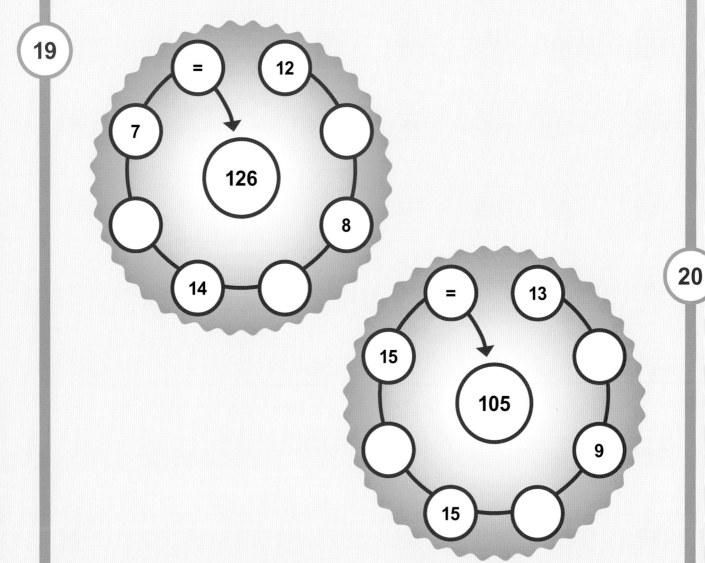

Tile Twister

Place the eight tiles into the puzzle grid so that all adjacent numbers on each tile match up. Tiles may be rotated through 360 degrees, but none may be flipped over. Write your answers on a separate sheet of paper.

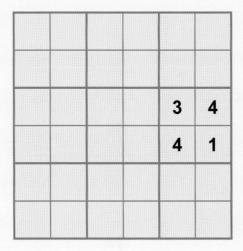

				3	4
				4	1

1	1
2	4

3	2
3	3

4	2
2	1

2	2
1	4

4	3
4	2

1	1
2	1

4	1
3	2

1	4
3	3

What's the Number?

In the diagram below, what number should replace the question mark? Write your answer on a separate sheet of paper.

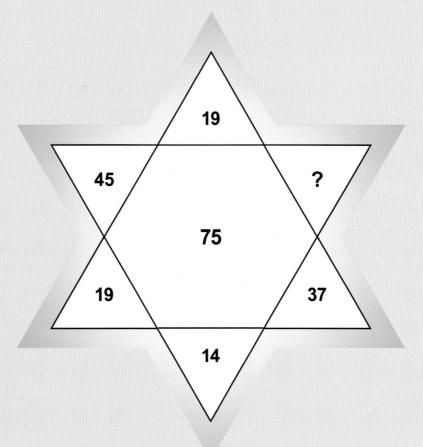

Symbol Math

Each symbol stands for a different number. In order to reach the correct total at the end of each row and column, what is the value of the circle, pentagon, square, and star? Write your answers on a separate sheet of paper.

23

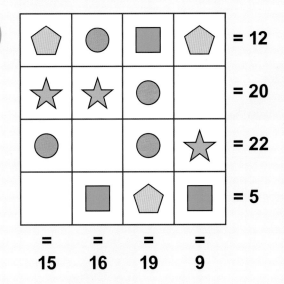

24

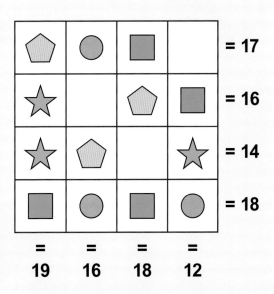

Number Path

Copy out this puzzle. Working from one square to another, horizontally or vertically (never diagonally), draw paths to pair up each set of two matching numbers. No path may be shared, and none may enter a square containing a number or part of another path. Write your answers on a separate sheet of paper.

5					9	4	6	7
3		3						
		8						
	5				4			
	2		2					
	9							
	6					7	10	
1	10							
1							8	

Tile Twister

Place the eight tiles into the puzzle grid so that all adjacent numbers on each tile match up. Tiles may be rotated through 360 degrees, but none may be flipped over. Write your answers on a separate sheet of paper.

26

		4	1		
		3	3		

3	2
1	1

2	3
4	2

2	3
1	3

1	4
3	2

4	4
2	3

3	1
4	1

3	1
1	4

3	1
1	2

Symbol Math

Each symbol stands for a different number. In order to reach the correct total at the end of each row and column, what is the value of the circle, pentagon, square, and star? Write your answers on a separate sheet of paper.

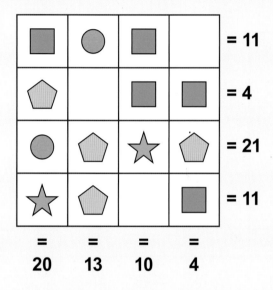

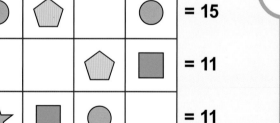

What's the Number?

In the diagram below, what number should replace the question mark? Write your answer on a separate sheet of paper.

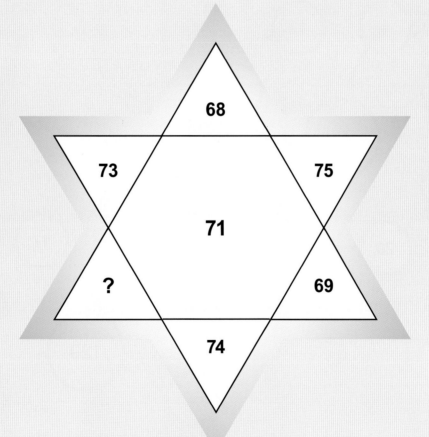

Circling In

The three empty circles should contain the symbols +, −, and x in some order, to make a series that leads to the number in the middle. Each symbol must be used once and calculations are made in a clockwise direction. Write your answers on a separate sheet of paper.

Symbol Math

Each symbol stands for a different number. In order to reach the correct total at the end of each row and column, what is the value of the circle, pentagon, square, and star? Write your answers on a separate sheet of paper.

32

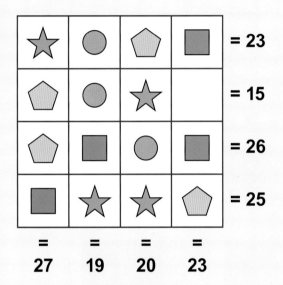

33

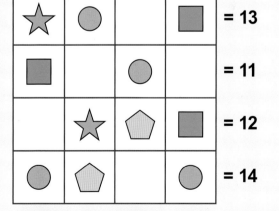

Making Arrangements

Arrange one each of the four numbers below, as well as one each of the symbols x (times), – (minus), and + (plus) in every row and column. You should arrive at the answer at the end of the row or column, making the calculations in the order in which they appear. Some are already in place. Write your answers on a separate sheet of paper.

34

3 4 7 9

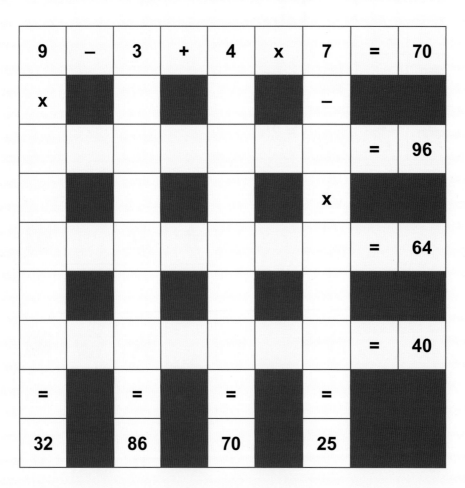

9	–	3	+	4	x	7	=	70
x						–		
							=	96
						x		
							=	64
							=	40
=		=		=		=		
32		86		70		25		

Number Crunch

Starting at the top left with the number provided, work down from one box to another, applying the mathematical instructions to your running total. Write your answers on a separate sheet of paper.

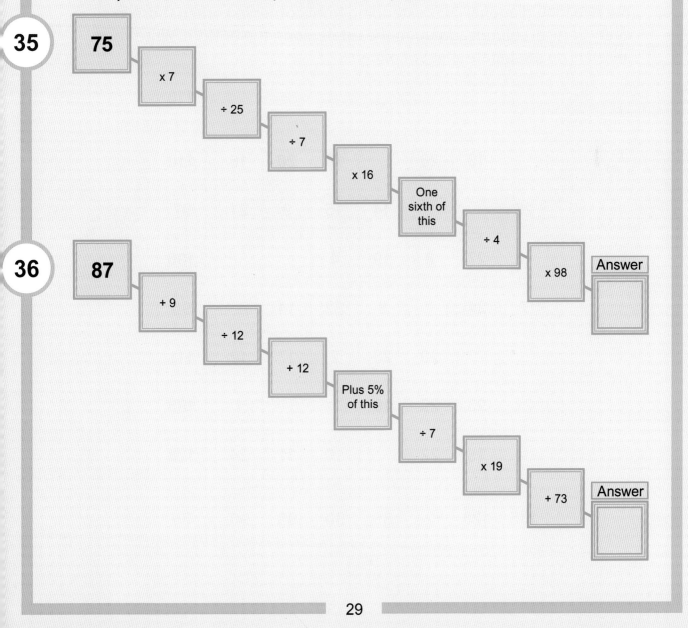

35

75 → x 7 → ÷ 25 → ÷ 7 → x 16 → One sixth of this → ÷ 4 → x 98 → Answer

36

87 → + 9 → ÷ 12 → + 12 → Plus 5% of this → ÷ 7 → x 19 → + 73 → Answer

Total Concentration

The blank squares below should contain whole numbers between 1 and 30 inclusive, any of which may occur more than once, or not at all. The numbers in every horizontal row add up to the totals on the right, as do the two long diagonal lines extending from corner to corner; those in every vertical column add up to the totals along the bottom. Write your answers on a separate sheet of paper.

37

							110
	19	26		18	20	16	**110**
25			14	15	9	21	**97**
18	27	8	19	4			**106**
7	24		8	22	14		**90**
		20	23	2	17	12	**111**
21	23	29	10			1	**108**
	15	22		16	11	24	**128**
135	**123**	**124**	**89**	**90**	**99**	**90**	**65**

One to Nine

Using the numbers one to nine, complete these six equations (three reading across and three reading downward). Every number is used once only, and one is already in place. Write your answers on a separate sheet of paper.

38

1 2 3 4 5 6 7 8 9

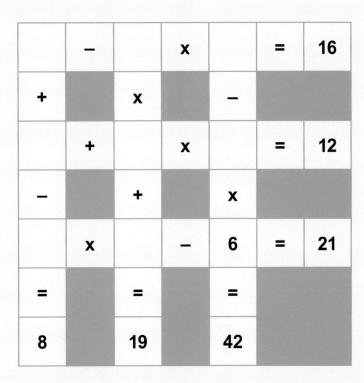

Circling In

The three empty circles should contain the symbols +, −, and x in some order, to make a series that leads to the number in the middle. Each symbol must be used once and calculations are made in a clockwise direction. Write your answers on a separate sheet of paper.

39

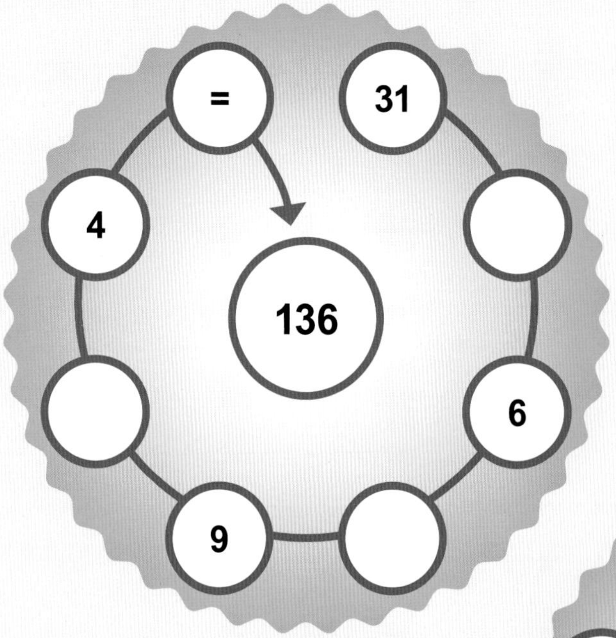

31

=

4

136

6

9

40

=

41

5

180

3

8

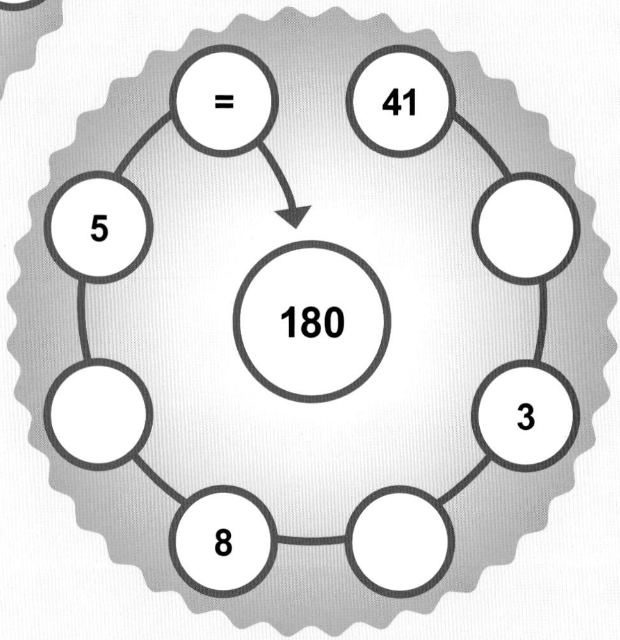

Symbol Math

Each symbol stands for a different number. In order to reach the correct total at the end of each row and column, what is the value of the circle, pentagon, square, and star? Write your answers on a separate sheet of paper.

41

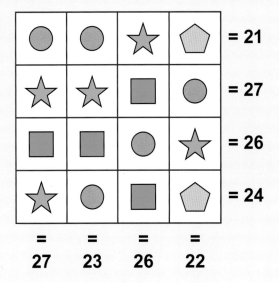

42

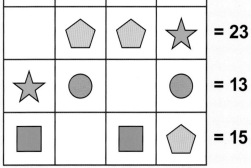

Tile Twister

Place the eight tiles into the puzzle grid so that all adjacent numbers on each tile match up. Tiles may be rotated through 360 degrees, but none may be flipped over. Write your answers on a separate sheet of paper.

43

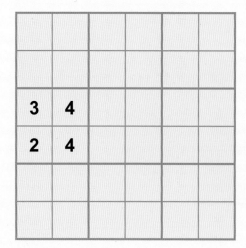

1	3
2	2

4	1
1	4

1	3
2	4

4	3
1	1

2	2
1	2

1	2
4	4

4	2
3	4

3	3
4	1

Number Crunch

Starting at the top left with the number provided, work down from one box to another, applying the mathematical instructions to your running total. Write your answers on a separate sheet of paper.

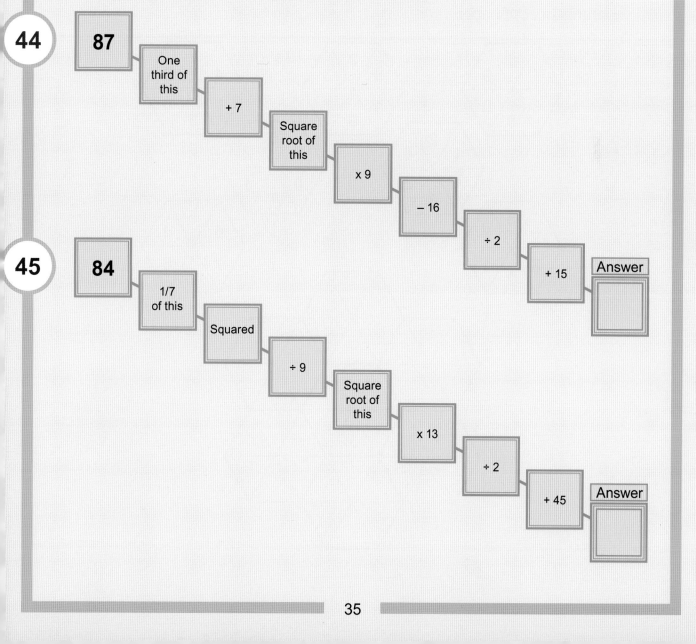

44

87 → One third of this → + 7 → Square root of this → x 9 → − 16 → ÷ 2 → + 15 → Answer

45

84 → 1/7 of this → Squared → ÷ 9 → Square root of this → x 13 → ÷ 2 → + 45 → Answer

Hexagony

Can you place the hexagons into the grid, so that where any hexagon touches another along a straight line, the number in both triangles is the same? No rotation of any hexagon is allowed! Write your answers on a separate sheet of paper.

What's the Number?

In the diagram below, what number should replace the question mark? Write your answer on a separate sheet of paper.

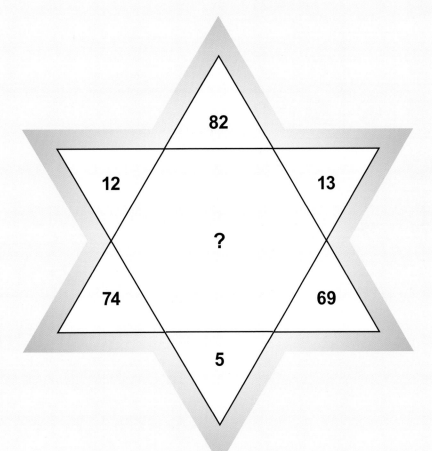

Symbol Math

Each symbol stands for a different number. In order to reach the correct total at the end of each row and column, what is the value of the circle, pentagon, square, and star? Write your answers on a separate sheet of paper.

48

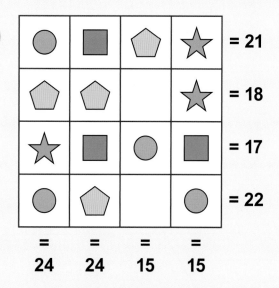

Row totals: = 21, = 18, = 17, = 22

Column totals:
= 24   = 24   = 15   = 15

49

Row totals: = 28, = 26, = 20, = 20

Column totals:
= 28   = 20   = 24   = 22

Word Puzzle

Find the Numbers

If you replace identical letters with the same number, which numbers do these letters stand for? Write your answer on a separate sheet of paper.

$$
\begin{array}{r}
\text{TRAMS} \\
\text{X} \qquad 4 \\
\hline
\text{SMART}
\end{array}
$$

1

3	2	2	1	1	2
1	2	2	4	4	3
1	2	2	4	4	3
2	3	3	4	4	1
2	3	3	4	4	1
1	1	1	2	2	1

2

Circle = 4, Pentagon = 8, Square = 3, Star = 7.

3

Circle = 2, Pentagon = 5, Square = 8, Star = 3.

4

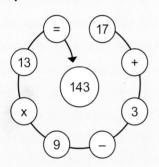

5

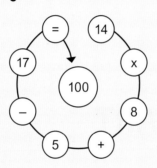

6

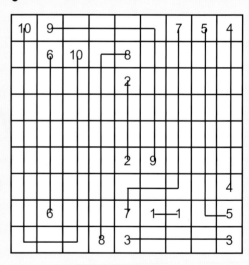

7

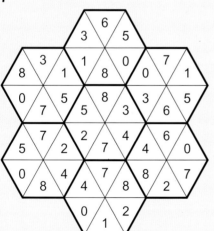

8

Circle = 9, Pentagon = 3, Square = 7, Star = 4.

9

Circle = 2, Pentagon = 8, Square = 1, Star = 6.

10

32 – Starting at the top and working clockwise,
7 – 4 = 3 x 4 = 12 – 4 = 8 x 4 = 32 x 4 = 128.

11

1	4	4	2	2	4
2	1	1	1	1	3
2	1	1	1	1	3
2	3	3	4	4	4
2	3	3	4	4	4
3	2	2	4	4	2

12

Circle = 7, Pentagon = 6, Square = 3, Star = 1.

13

Circle = 8, Pentagon = 1, Square = 7, Star = 4.

14

9	–	1	+	4	=	12
–		+		x		
3	+	7	x	5	=	50
+		x		–		
2	x	6	+	8	=	20
=		=		=		
8		48		12		

15

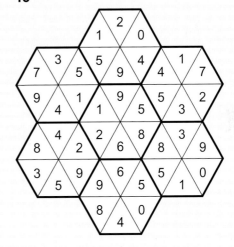

16

Circle = 7, Pentagon = 9, Square = 5, Star = 3.

17

Circle = 4, Pentagon = 8, Square = 3, Star = 5.

Solutions

18

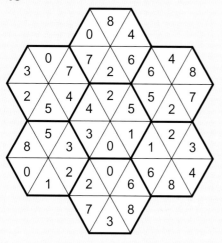

19

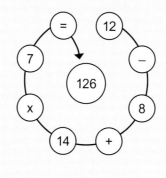

20

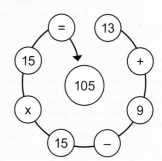

21

4	3	3	3	3	1
4	2	2	3	3	4
4	2	2	3	3	4
2	1	1	4	4	1
2	1	1	4	4	1
1	1	1	2	2	2

22

16 – The star is made of two overlapping triangles, and the three numbers in the points of each triangle total the central number.

23

Circle = 8, Pentagon = 1, Square = 2, Star = 6.

24

Circle = 4, Pentagon = 8, Square = 5, Star = 3.

25

26

4	4	4	1	1	2
2	3	3	3	3	1
2	3	3	3	3	1
4	2	2	1	1	4
4	2	2	1	1	4
1	3	3	1	1	3

27

Circle = 9, Pentagon = 2, Square = 1, Star = 8.

28

Circle = 3, Pentagon = 9, Square = 2, Star = 6.

29

70 – Working clockwise from the top, 68 + 7 = 75
– 6 = 69 + 5 = 74 – 4 = 70 + 3 = 73 – 2 = 71.

30

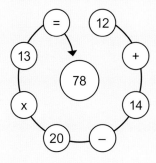

31

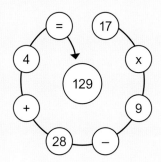

32

Circle = 3, Pentagon = 7, Square = 8, Star = 5.

33

Circle = 5, Pentagon = 4, Square = 6, Star = 2.

34

9	–	3	+	4	x	7	=	70
x		+		+		–		
4	+	7	x	9	–	3	=	96
–		x		–		x		
7	x	9	–	3	+	4	=	64
+		–		x		+		
3	+	4	x	7	–	9	=	40
=		=		=		=		
32		86		70		25		

43

35

75 x 7 = 525, 525 ÷ 25 = 21, 21 ÷ 7 = 3, 3 x 16 = 48, 48 ÷ 6 = 8, 8 ÷ 4 = 2, 2 x 98 = 196

36

87 + 9 = 96, 96 ÷ 12 = 8, 8 + 12 = 20, 20 + 1 = 21, 21 ÷ 7 = 3, 3 x 19 = 57, 57 + 73 = 130

37

							110
6	19	26	5	18	20	16	110
25	6	7	14	15	9	21	97
18	27	8	19	4	17	13	106
7	24	12	8	22	14	3	90
28	9	20	23	2	17	12	111
21	23	29	10	13	11	1	108
30	15	22	10	16	11	24	128
135	123	124	89	90	99	90	65

38

4	–	2	x	8	=	16
+		x		–		
7	+	5	x	1	=	12
–		+		x		
3	x	9	–	6	=	21
=		=		=		
8		19		42		

39

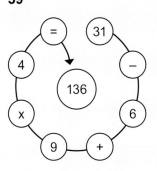

40

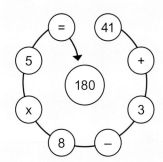

41

Circle = 4, Pentagon = 5, Square = 7, Star = 8.

42

Circle = 2, Pentagon = 7, Square = 4, Star = 9.

43

1	1	1	4	4	3
3	4	4	1	1	3
3	4	4	1	1	3
2	4	4	2	2	2
2	4	4	2	2	2
4	3	3	1	1	2

44

87 ÷ 3 = 29, 29 + 7 = 36, square root of 36 = 6, 6 x 9 = 54, 54 − 16 = 38, 38 ÷ 2 = 19, 19 + 15 = 34

84 ÷ 7 = 12, 12^2 = 144, 144 ÷ 9 = 16, square root of 16 = 4, 4 x 13 = 52, 52 ÷ 2 = 26, 26 + 45 = 71

46

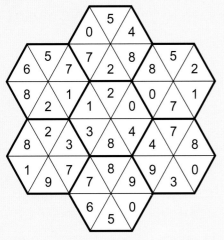

47

62 – Working clockwise from the top, 82 − 13 = 69 + 5 = 74 − 12 = 62.

48

Circle = 7, Pentagon = 8, Square = 4, Star = 2.

49

Circle = 4, Pentagon = 6, Square = 2, Star = 8.

50

21978 x 4 = 87912

Glossary

adjacent   Close to or—more commonly—next to.

calculation   The use of math to find a solution.

clockwise   A circular movement that goes in the same direction that a clock's hands travel.

column   A line of objects that goes straight up and down.

concentration   Thinking very hard and examining every possibility.

diagonal   Moving in a slanted direction, halfway between straight across and straight down.

diagram   A drawing or outline to explain how something works.

grid   A display of crisscrossed lines.

hexagon   A six-sided object.

horizontal   A direction that is straight across.

inclusive   Including both ends of a series (two to five inclusive means 2, 3, 4, and 5).

matching   Exactly the same as.

pentagon   A five-sided object.

rotate   Travel in a circular motion.

rotation   Circular motion.

row   A line of objects that goes straight across.

square root   A number that, if multiplied by itself, produces the original number (3 is the square root of 9; 4 is the square root of 16).

squared   When a number is multiplied by itself (3 squared = 3 x 3 = 9).

symbol   An image that represents something else.

vertical   A direction that is straight up and down.

whole number   A number that has no decimals (4 is a whole number; 4.3 is not a whole number).

Further Information

For more information:

Consortium for Mathematics (COMAP)
175 Middlesex Turnpike, Bedford, MA 01730
(800) 772-6627 http://www.comap.com/index.html
COMAP is a nonprofit organization whose mission is to improve mathematics education for students of all ages. It works with teachers, students, and business people to create learning environments where mathematics is used to investigate and model real issues in our world.

MATHCOUNTS Foundation
1420 King Street, Alexandria, VA 22314
(703) 299-9006 https://mathcounts.org/sslpage.aspx
MATHCOUNTS is a national enrichment, club, and competition program that promotes middle school mathematics achievement. To secure America's global competitiveness, MATHCOUNTS inspires excellence, confidence, and curiosity in U.S. middle school students through fun and challenging math programs.

National Council of Teachers of Mathematics (NCTM)
906 Association Drive, Reston, VA 20191-1502
(703) 620-9840 http://www.nctm.org
The NCTM is a public voice of mathematics education supporting teachers to ensure equitable mathematics learning of the highest quality for all students through vision, leadership, professional development and research.

Web Sites

Due to the changing nature of Internet links, Rosen Publishing has developed an online list of Web sites related to the subject of this book. This site is updated regularly. Please use this link to access this list:

http://www.rosenlinks.com/msw/symb

Further Reading

Abramson., Marcie F. *Painless Math Word Problems.* New York, NY: Barron's Educational Series, 2010.

Fisher, Richard W. *Mastering Essential Math Skills: 20 Minutes a Day to Success (Book Two: Middle Grades/High School).* Los Gatos, CA: Math Essentials, 2007.

Lewis, Barry. *Help Your Kids With Math: A Visual Problem Solver for Kids and Parents.* New York, NY: DK Publishing, 2010.

Overholt, James and Laurie Kincheloe. *Math Wise! Over 100 Hands-On Activities That Promote Real Math Understanding.* New York, NY: Jossey-Bass, 2010.

Index